Annie Fredj is an experienced teacher, having worked with hundreds of children in both Europe and Australia over her career. She holds qualifications in English and social sciences, and is passionate about helping children thrive. Annie is a survivor of domestic violence, which has inspired and informed her writing. *Safe Adults, Hard Adults* is her first published work. Annie enjoys volunteering in a mum's group, playing music, and spending time with her loved ones.

Independently Published

Cover design by Kaitlyn Rasmussen

First edition

ISBN: 978-0-6458479-0-1

For my God who sustains me,

For my son who motivates me,

For caring adults who seek,

And for all the children whose voices are silent.

Contents

Introduction for Adults

"How do I explain it to my kids?" is the question that led to this book being written. With a background in English literature, and early language development and education, my initial aim was to simply brainstorm a few age-appropriate key words to help talk about things with my own son. After all, if you have the right words to talk about problems, then they become much easier to solve. I found plenty of information online aimed at adults, but frustratingly little hands-on information for children.

Children are too frequently the silent victims in family dramas, who do not yet have the right vocabulary to express their thoughts and feelings, especially in the face of gaslighting, manipulation, and fear. This can lead to their emotional and psychological needs flying under the radar. While connecting with other parents on the same journey, I realised that the question of "how can I explain this to my kids?" is a constant struggle for many, and that is when my personal notes became the bones of this book. I hope it makes a positive difference for you all.

Domestic Violence (DV) is much more common than most people want to believe. In Australia (where I live) 11.8% of adults have experienced DV in a relationship. Children are often the witnesses to these events, which fall under the umbrella of Family Violence. The World Health Organisation (WHO) state on their website that "globally it is estimated that up to 1 billion children aged 2-17 years, have experienced physical, sexual, or emotional violence or neglect in the past year."[1] Those are staggering numbers.

Although this book is not specifically about Narcissistic Personality Disorder (NPD), it focuses on the effects that general narcissistic and other harmful behaviours have on the children who experience it. Narcissistic Personality Disorder (NPD) occurs in about 0.5% of the population, but we all have narcissistic tendencies. Whilst we explore the ways children are victims, the focus is on children finding ways to express themselves, develop an understanding of the complex relationships in their lives, and to start creating healthy coping mechanisms. This book is child-centric and healing focused.

Without pointing fingers, vilifying, or using a bunch of complex psychological terminology, this book helps kids work things out for themselves. It is worded in the first person, so they know it is for

---

1. WHO website as of 18/7/2023 https://www.who.int/news-room/fact-sheets/detail/violence-against-children

them. The language used leaves it open to interpret the gender, age, and relationships involved. Some of the material may be triggering for young children, so I highly recommend adults read the book alone first, and if there are any parts that may not be relevant for your child you can skip them. Notably, I do not focus on substance abuse, mental disorders, or anything that is centred on the issues of the Hard Adult.

This is a book to read together with your child, in a calm and safe environment. Take your time with each section, talking things through together. At the end of each section there are questions for the children to reflect on their lives, helping to start a conversation. As parents, we are often focused on finding fast solutions to the issues, but as you read together, try focusing on being emotionally present and understanding what your child feels. Healing starts with seeing and accepting. It is not light reading; the topics are tough, the questions are searching, so be prepared to even it out with some light-hearted activities.

Do you find it difficult to talk with your child about these issues? You are not alone! Here are some concepts to think about:

Intergenerational trauma means that working on your own mental health is critical. You are the role model on self-regulation, anger management, empathy, and healthy attachments. Kids will naturally do as you do and not as you say. Owning your own imperfections and putting work into your own healing journey is one of the bravest and most important things you can ever do, for both yourself and your family. Healing is a journey you are on together. Let them see your successes and failures and grow together.

Be present, focus on listening to their words and witness their emotions. The way children may make you feel can be a reflection of how they themselves feel. Stay conscious of that. Sit with those feelings together, acknowledge them, and give time to co-regulate with your child back to a secure space before moving on. That may mean going through the book really slowly, but that is totally ok. True healing cannot be rushed.

Ask them "How can I support you right now?"

Do not invalidate their experience with thoughts like "others have it worse than you," "it is better off this way," "what does not kill you makes you stronger," or "you do not get more than you can handle in life."

Validate their experience and encourage them to open up further; "I can see that was very hard for you. Can you tell me more about it?"

Make sure they know that you are there for them going forward. It is good to remember that they want to be seen, heard, and understood.

The quality of your relationship is the focus and that will in turn bring the healing, not the other way around.

Remember that internal change happens faster than external results, and that it will take time to notice changes.

For some, physical touch can be healing. Hugs, rocking back and forth together, a gentle face massage, or a gentle back rub can help with feeling calm and safe. Creating the right head space before starting a reading session can really help.

The goal of this book is twofold; firstly, to help kids understand how to navigate the relationship with the Hard Adult(s) in their life, and also to give them age-appropriate terminology they can use to express themselves to psychologists, social workers, teachers, and anyone else vested in their safety. This book should not be used instead of therapy, and I highly encourage finding the right support systems for yourself and your children.

Introduction for Kids

Some adults around me are really loving and caring, and I feel safe with them. They are safe because they take on the job of looking after me. Even when they may get grumpy and make mistakes, they are still there to support me. These people are called my Safe Adults. I also have someone (or perhaps more than one person) in my life who is more confusing, and who can be difficult to understand and be around.

This person is a Hard Adult, because it can be hard to understand how they behave, hard to understand how they make me feel, and hard to know what they want from me. Sometimes Hard Adults are so confusing that I do not even know for sure if they are a Hard Adult.

Safe Adults and Hard Adults does not mean good adults and bad adults. Nobody is all good, and nobody is all bad. These names are there to help me understand what is happening and help me make positive choices in my relationships with these adults.

This book will help me learn the difference between Safe Adults and Hard Adults. It will help me understand more about what Hard Adults do, how I feel about them, and what I can do to get help. This is not a regular story book, instead it talks about situations that might be similar to my life, some stories other kids have gone through, and some questions to help me think about the important people in my life. This is a book for me.

Chapter 1

Things They Do

My Safe Adults are people around me who I can trust because of how they behave. Their actions show that they care about me and they can help me when I need it. They do not just **say** they love me, they really **show** they love me. For example, they protect me from danger and help me feel safe. They ask me to talk about my feelings and they respect my feelings, so that when we are together I can be myself. I do not have to pretend to be different so they like me.

Safe Adults tell the truth and keep their promises, and I can usually talk to them about my problems. They are open to talking about difficult things and they regularly ask me how I feel and what I think about things. I can tell that they care about my responses.

Safe Adults are ok with me saying "no" to something. Sometimes, when Safe Adults feel sad or angry, they may shout or cry as they have big feelings, but I still feel safe with them. Their anger is not pushed onto me. When they do make mistakes they apologise to me, and I can see that they are really sorry and not just saying it.

When things go wrong in life, Safe Adults think about how to solve the problem instead of getting angry at me. They do their best at communicating well with others, and making careful decisions that include me in a caring way. They respect that I am myself, and do not try to change me into someone I do not want to be. They trust me to learn and try things, and they are supportive when I make mistakes. They let me be a kid and do not expect me to solve their problems. They know that adult problems are their responsibility and not mine.

Activity Time

- Who helps me with my feelings and worries?
- Who helps me be seen, heard, and understood?
- How do they show me they love me?
- How do I know I can trust them?
- How do they behave when I tell them about my worries?
- How do they behave when I do something wrong?

Example

Once there was a girl called Aaliyah. Her parents were going through a divorce, they spent a lot of time shouting at each other, and were often impatient with her as well. Aaliyah hated all the shouting, so she often hid in her room listening to music with her headphones on. But every night her dad would go to her room and ask about her day. No matter how messy things got, he made sure that Aaliyah had some time to talk about her feelings. Listening patiently to her problems, he would help her come up with ideas about how to make things easier for her.

Eventually her parents moved into different houses, and on days that Aaliyah did not see her dad he would video chat with her and ask how she was feeling. He would usually make it to her sports matches and school events and cheer her on. When the divorce was done and he had calmed down, he apologised to Aaliyah about how impatient and grumpy he was with her during that difficult time and said that in the future he would try his best to not be impatient with her just because he was having a bad day.

Activity Time

- What did Aaliyah's dad do wrong?
- What did Aaliyah's dad do right?
- Is he a Safe Adult who Aaliyah can trust?

Hard Adults are people around me who I struggle to trust because of how they behave. What they say and how they act do not match, and that can be so confusing! This is really hard because I love them and want them to love me. There are three different ways that Hard Adults do things that can make life difficult.

The first thing is when they act in a way that makes me feel like they do not care enough. The second thing is when they make me do things that I do not like to do. And the third thing is when I see them do bad things to a Safe Adult or somebody else around me.

A Hard Adult may not like to help me with my problems when I am with them. They may get upset when I ask for help, or annoyed when they have to do something for me. I can recognise a Hard Adult because they do not always respect my feelings. For example, they may say they love me, but they do not always behave like they love me, or they ignore me when I really need them to be there for me.

When things go wrong, Hard Adults might blame other people or me but will not accept that they are responsible for the things they have done. They sometimes even stop talking to me and including me in things we normally do together. They may disappear for a long time, then come back and make life messy again.

Activity Time

- Is there anyone in my life who does some of these things?
- How do they behave when I tell them about my worries?
  ignores it
- How do they behave when I do something wrong?
- How does their behaviour make me feel?
  sad, upset, angry, miss mom

Example

Antonio has an uncle who he loves very much. His uncle likes to take him to sports events, lets him eat junk food, and he can watch whatever he wants on the T.V. But Antonio's uncle also does stuff that makes Antonio feel really uncomfortable. One day they were going to go to an outdoor sports event together, and his uncle was busy packing all their stuff in the car while Antonio had breakfast.

When they had arrived, Antonio realised that his uncle had forgotten to pack his jumper. Antonio was shivering with cold and could not enjoy the game at all, but when he told his uncle how cold he was, his uncle said it was his fault, and he was stupid for not packing the jumper. His uncle refused to grab a blanket from the car and told Antonio he has to learn his lesson by staying cold.

Antonio did not have a choice, so he sat there the whole time feeling miserable. On the way home in the car his uncle complained that it was no fun to spend time together with Antonio when he was grumpy. He said he will not take Antonio to any more events unless he starts behaving.

Activity Time

- What could Antonio's uncle have done to help him?
  get a blanket
- How did Antonio's uncle treat his feelings?
  like it was all his fault
- How did Antonio's uncle behave when things went wrong? he let him be cold. made things worse.
- How is Antonio's story similar to mine?

One of the big reasons Hard Adults can be so hard to be around is because they find it difficult to respect my thoughts and feelings. I know how important it is to be kind and respectful to others, so it is fair to have kindness and respect shown towards me as well. Being kind and respectful includes looking after each other's bodies, feelings, and belongings.

Hard Adults may hurt my body, my feelings, or my stuff. They can also do this to other people, which hurts me to see. It is important to remember that **I have the right to feel safe**. It is normal for kids to have safety around their bodies, feelings, and belongings, and I deserve to have that, too.

Hard Adults might lie about important things. They do not apologise when they make a mistake, or only apologise to get something they want or to feel better about themselves. They may not accept me as I am, and they want to change me in ways I do not like. They sometimes say things are my fault but I am not sure it is true. They may also use threats to make me or others around me do what they want.

Activity Time

- Is there anyone in my life who does some of these things?
- How do they behave when I tell them about my worries?
- How do they behave when I do something wrong?
- What do my feelings tell me about this relationship?

Example

Shanae's dad got angry a lot. He would punch the walls, and hurt people too. He did not hit her though- he would say things like "If you do not do as I ask then I will hurt your mum." Shanae tried to be as good as she could, but it wasn't always enough to keep him happy, and he would hurt her mum, making sure that Shanae saw and heard it happen. She wanted to talk to her mum about it, but something stopped her from talking. What if talking about it would get her in more trouble?

Finally, one day her dad did what she feared most- he went into Shanae's room, threw her stuff against the wall and then hurt her. Shanae was even more scared of saying something. Later, her dad said sorry to her and forced her to give him a hug. She did not want to hug him at that time, but he made her. It felt wrong. Her dad said "I wish you were more like me and then I would not have to do this to you." Shanae felt like she could never be good enough for her dad, and that made her really sad, because she really wanted him to love her just the way she was.

Activity Time

- In what ways was Shanae's dad not respectful to her?
- Should Shanae have to change to be like her dad? Why?
- When Shanae's dad apologised to her was it a real apology? What did he really want?
- How do I behave when I am scared of a person in my life?
- How is Shanae's story similar to mine?

I am not the only one who finds Hard Adults hard. They can be really hard for other kids and adults as well. Some things Hard Adults might do include things like keeping bad secrets from a Safe Adult or other adults, or they might bully or hurt a Safe Adult. They may keep me away from a Safe Adult. For example, maybe I should be spending some weekends with the Safe Adult, and the Hard Adult does not let me go, or they could stop me from being able to text or video chat with a Safe Adult.

They could be listening when I talk with a Safe Adult so I cannot say what I want to. They could say mean things to me and to other people about my Safe Adult that hurt my feelings, or try to stop me from trusting a Safe Adult. They may lie about things to make others look bad and make themselves look good. Sometimes Hard Adults will do the good things that Safe Adults do, but Safe Adults will not do the mean things that Hard Adults do. It is ok for me to be upset, angry, scared, and sad about the hard things they do. It is ok and important for me to talk about these things with Safe Adults.

Activity Time

- Is there anyone in my life who does some of these things?
- How do they behave when I tell them about my worries?
- How do they behave when I do something wrong?
- How does their behaviour make me feel?

Example

Kashvi was supposed to spend every second weekend with her dad at his house along with her little brother, Arin. While at his house they wanted to talk to their mum on the phone, but their dad would not let them. He said their mum was too busy making friends with other people, and that she "did not really care" about them anyway.

That felt wrong to Kashvi, but she was too afraid to argue with him. Arin got upset and cried, which made their dad really angry. He shouted at Arin, saying "Mummy does not love you. Stop being such a baby. I hate it when you cry!" When it was time to go back to their mum's house Kashvi's dad did not take them. He said that mum did not want Kashvi and Arin anymore because she was a bad person. He made Kashvi and Arin go to a new school near his house, and they could not see their friends anymore.

Kashvi was very upset, because she knew that things were not right, but she did not know what was really going on. Soon after all this happened, their dad made Kashvi call his girlfriend 'mum,' which Kashvi did not want at all. It felt like their dad was trying to make them forget their real mum, and they got in trouble if they did not do it.

Activity Time

- Why is it important for Kashvi and Arin to be able to talk to their mum?
- How did Arin feel when his dad shouted at him?
- What does crying mean? Should we let ourselves and others cry?
- What was the reason Kashvi's dad said the mean things about her mum?
- Kashvi cannot talk to her mum or other Safe Adults at her old school. Who can she go to for help?
- Kashvi does not want to call her dad's girlfriend 'mum.' Why is that so important? Should she be allowed to choose what to call her?

Practice Saying

- I do not need to change myself to make other people happy.
- It is normal for adults to treat me, others, and themselves with respect.
- It is normal for an adult's words and behaviours to match up.

How people behave says a lot about how they think and feel. Safe Adults care about me, and their actions show that. Hard Adults are more confusing, because what they say and what they do doesn't always match. A good way to spot a Hard Adult is to look at the way they respect my feelings, my body, and my stuff and other people's bodies, feelings, and stuff.

Another way is looking at how they deal with problems. Hard Adults often blame other people, and only say sorry if it makes things better for them. They do not like to be responsible, even though they are the adults. Hard Adults may also lie or create other problems with the Safe Adults in my life. I can now watch a Hard Adult and pay attention to these things. What do they do in my life?

Chapter 2

How They Make Me Feel

The way that other people treat me can change how I feel. When I am with a Safe Adult they help me feel safe with them because I can trust them to look after me. They make sure I have what I need (like food, clothes, and a home), and I feel comfortable being close to them.

Safe Adults make me feel happy, because they listen to me when I talk about my feelings, they care when I am upset, and they do thoughtful things to bring me joy. I do not always get everything I want, but I know they are looking after me. Safe Adults help me feel loved because I know that even if I do something wrong they will still be there for me. I know that I am important to them.

Activity Time

- What do my Safe Adults do to make me feel safe?
- What do my Safe Adults do to make me feel happy?
- What do my Safe Adults do to make me feel loved?

When bad things happen around me it can make big feelings happen inside me. I may be scared about something that has happened or I worry might happen. There could be things going on that I do not understand, and it makes the adults around me upset, and that scares me. When something like this happens it is the right time to ask for help.

A Hard Adult can make me feel happy, loved and special some of the time. They might buy me nice gifts, or do really exciting things with me. Maybe they let me do things that Safe Adults would not let me do, and that is exciting! Just because they are a difficult person I can still love them. It is okay to love a Hard Adult, and I should not feel guilty for caring about them.

I might feel guilt or shame about bad things that Hard Adults have done, and that what happened is my fault. Someone may even tell me that it *is* my fault. Hard Adults may tell me that I am not allowed to tell other people about the bad things, and I do not want to disappoint them or upset them. I could feel like keeping bad secrets will help me stay safe or loved.

I might feel ashamed of all the bad things that have happened, and may not want other people to know how I am feeling or how others that I love are behaving. When a Hard Adult does something bad it is **not** my fault, even if they say that it *is*. I do **not** have to feel ashamed or guilty for something that someone else did or something they made me do. If something bad happens to me then Safe Adults **want to know**, and it is **okay to tell them.**

I might want to pretend a bad thing did not happen at all and refuse to talk about it. I could try my best not to think about it. I might think "maybe, if I ignore it, then it will go away." But somehow it just makes me feel worse and worse. If I keep all my big feelings stuck inside then they just grow and make my life a lot sadder. Nobody deserves that!

For some people big feelings keep growing bigger and bigger, then pop like a giant balloon. That could look like a lot of uncontrolled movement, anger, words, and tears. Safe Adults care about how I feel, and they are ok with me telling them my worries. The more they understand what is wrong, the better they can help me.

I could feel very lonely, like nobody else in the world understands what has happened to me. I may not always feel safe when I am with a Hard Adult. Sometimes I feel like I am in danger or someone else is in danger, or I feel alone because I can't trust the Hard Adult to be there for me. I am worried that I might say or do something that will make them angry.

Lots of kids have Hard Adults in their lives, so I am not alone in my worries, and there are lots of adults who understand exactly what is going on.

It is not okay for Hard Adults to put me or others in danger, and **I should be able to trust the adults in my life**. If there is someone in my life who behaves like a Hard Adult, it is okay to talk about it with people who can help me. **I am not alone**.

I may be angry and want to shout and break things. I might want to hurt the person who hurt me, or make them realise what they did wrong and apologise to me. Maybe I am really upset that someone did not agree with me on something. When unfair things happen it is normal for me to be upset about it, but I am the one that needs to choose- will I respond with anger, or can I learn to be gentle and forgiving?

Bad things happen to everyone, but not everyone behaves badly. I can learn to use my angry energy in good ways, like doing sport, singing, dancing, or doing something else that helps me calm down. I can talk to Safe Adults to help me find the best ideas for me.

Maybe I feel really confused about what happened and how I feel about it. These are all such big feelings, and they can be so strong. It can be hard to know exactly how I feel about everything. Good feelings can be mixed up with bad ones, the truth can be mixed up with lies- it is hard to know what to think! That is okay. Most adults can also be confused about all their big feelings, just like me. It is completely normal to not understand everything that is happening in my life, and it is okay to ask for help with it.

Example

Haoyo had a complicated relationship with his mum. She was great at making jokes, playing games, taking him to the skate park after school, and letting him play computer games with his friends. But she did not do things that other adults would do, like taking him shopping when his shoes got too small and painful for his feet. When he reminded her she complained about not having enough money, and then he felt guilty about wanting new shoes and making her stressed out. She talked about money a lot, and Haoyo felt bad about asking for things he wanted.

He started cleaning cars and walking people's dogs to make a bit of pocket money so he could afford to buy shoes and have some lunch money. His mum thought it was a great idea, told him he was a smart kid, and then she refused to buy him clothes as well. Haoyo felt really upset and lonely, like nobody would understand how hard things were for him.

It was not fair, but he felt alone with his problem. He was getting angry at his mum, because he felt that she should be more responsible, but she was only around for the fun stuff. Haoyo was really confused, because he loved his mum so much, and he thought if he helps out a bit she will be more responsible too, but things just kept getting worse.

Activity time

- It feels nice to have a parent who takes care of me, but how would it feel if they stopped acting like a responsible adult?
- Why is Haoyo feeling like things are not fair?
- Why is it so important that adults in my life are responsible for looking after me?
- Haoyo's mum loves him, but is still a Hard Adult. What does she need to change to be a Safe Adult?
- Is Haoyo able to change his mum's behaviour?

The Hard Adult can also make it feel like my feelings do not matter. Because of this I think I need to change myself to make the Hard Adult happy. Maybe if I am good enough for them, then they will see it and things will get better. Maybe if I just try hard enough then I can fix the problem. The good news is, **I do not have to change myself to be good enough!**

Hard Adults might find it hard to love me as I am, but that is **their** problem and not mine. It is not my job to make them happy. It is not my job to fix their problems. **All** adults are responsible for their own feelings and problems- **that is part of the job of being an adult**.

Something kids like me struggle with, is feeling guilty about the relationships in my life. For example, one adult can say really horrible things to me about another adult who I love. They may also say mean things about other kids to make me feel jealous or upset. An adult may try to use me to get another adult to do something they do not want to do. **This is not okay**.

Adults are responsible for solving adult problems with each other, and adults are responsible for their feelings about other adults. It is okay for me to love all the adults in my life, and it is okay for me to refuse to get involved in their mess. If there is an issue I can talk to a Safe Adult about it.

Another important truth for me to understand is that adults in my life should not be using **my** feelings to decide how **they** feel about themselves. For example, a Safe Adult would be able to listen to me telling them things they do not like or do not agree with without taking it personally (obviously I would try to be as kind about it as possible).

Safe Adults are able to accept when I say "no" to something they want me to do. Just because my opinion or decisions do not match with theirs they can accept it.

Hard Adults cannot. They see my choices as a personal attack on them, and they let **my** choices hurt **their** feelings, even if my choices are valid and not meant to hurt them. I could be the nicest person on the planet and they would still be offended. Often in these situations, Hard Adults will focus on their feelings rather than problem solving, or blame me for things that have gone wrong, even though the thing they blame me for is **their responsibility**. They may also become angry at others and blame others.

Activity Time

- What has happened to make me feel confused, scared or angry?
- What has happened to make me feel shame or guilt?
- What do I usually do when I am feeling these bad feelings?
- What do I do to avoid problems with the Hard Adult?
- What is stopping me from talking about all these feelings with a Safe Adult?

Example

Min and her sisters often visited her grandpa and grandma. They would stay with them for a few nights while their parents went away. Min loved listening to grandma's stories and playing in the garden. But grandpa was a Hard Adult who made Min's life quite difficult. It was like he did not love her the same as her sisters, and he would say things like "If you were a boy it would be better. The oldest should be a boy." That made Min feel guilty and that she wasn't good enough.

One time Min was so upset that she did not want to eat dinner, and Grandpa said "You're just going to stay a skinny and weak girl. You make me look bad!" Min felt really sad, and also a bit angry that he always picked on her and never her sisters. It was not fair! Min became jealous of her sisters because they were treated better and had a lot more fun when staying with their grandparents.

Min started to do things she did not really want to do, like extra chores around the house, hoping that it would be enough to make Grandpa love her, but he just kept saying mean things to her. No matter how hard she tried he was never happy.

Activity time

- Does Min need to change to be good enough? Why?
- What makes Min's grandpa a Hard Adult?
- Are Min's sisters responsible for making things better?

There is something else really important to know about feelings. **My feelings are not who I am**. I feel my feelings, but they are not part of me. They are just a reflection of what is happening outside of me. I can have feelings about what is happening right now, and also through memories of things that happened before. For example, if I hear my parents fighting it can make me feel scared or worried right now.

I could also remember back to something bad that happened to me a long time ago and even though I am not in danger now I could still feel scared or worried. Feelings can trick me into thinking there is something wrong even when the danger is long gone. It is good for me to remember that.

Negative feelings can sometimes have positive uses. For example, anger can help me realise that I am not being treated fairly, or fear can let me know that there is something which needs my attention.

I could feel like I have very little control over my own life. Adults make all the big decisions, and I can end up with a lot of big feelings inside me. Sometimes it feels really horrible. But; I can remember that those feelings are not a part of me. I can feel angry, but that does not mean I am an angry person. It is just a feeling inside me, which means I can tell it to go away! I can think about feelings growing legs and walking away.

Goodbye fear, I do not need you. I am stronger without you! Goodbye worrying, you take up too much space in my mind! Goodbye anger, you cause too many problems! My mind is my castle, and I can choose who to let in. Feelings are a guest, not the homeowner. The world around me can be full of all sorts of bad things, but those bad things do not deserve a place in my heart and mind.

Practice saying

- Adults are responsible for their own feelings and problems.
- I am allowed to be angry, but it is not okay to hurt others.
- My feelings are not who I am. I can choose to let go of feelings I do not wish to keep.

Looking at my feelings is a useful way to help me work out who are Hard Adults, and how they change the way I feel. Unlike my Safe Adults, they do not always give me the feeling of being safe and well looked after. They can blame me for things that have happened, making me feel ashamed and guilty. Life with them can feel unfair, making me feel upset and angry. Sometimes my feelings are confused, with good and bad feelings mixing together.

I can remember that feelings are things that come and go, but are not actually part of who I am. They do not decide the sort of person I am. Hard Adults can make feelings very complicated. I can learn to separate how I feel about the Hard Adult from how they make me feel. Hard Adults can be funny, give great gifts, and be really sweet, but if they are also doing all sorts of Hard Adult behaviours it is important for me to understand that that is also who they are.

Now I understand that it is not normal to live with these sorts of feelings. This book will also help me to understand ways to deal with a Hard Adult in my life, so let's keep learning!

Chapter 3

What They Ask Me to Do

As a kid it feels like adults are telling me what to do **all the time**! Maybe they ask me to do things that I do not really enjoy doing like cleaning up or brushing my teeth, but those are normal things to ask a kid to do. Safe Adults ask normal things from me like:

- Asking me to be honest
- Asking me to try my best
- Asking me to do my fair share of helping
- Asking me to take part in safe events
- Asking me to be respectful

Activity Time

- Who are the Safe Adults in my life?
- What do they do that helps me know they are really safe for me?
- How do Safe Adults respond when I do not do as they ask?

Hard Adults can do the things that Safe Adults do, but they may also mix in some behaviours that are not ok. There are lots of things this could include, so they are organised into three lists. This first list looks at what Hard Adults may ask me to do about my feelings:

- They tell me how I should feel and what I should think.
- They use guilt to make me do things I do not want to do.
- They make me responsible for adult feelings.
- They push me to spend time with them or do something for them by making me or someone else feel guilty or responsible.
- They tell me not to cry.
- If I cry or show any feelings they do not like they get upset and blame me.
- I feel like I have to fit into their expectations instead of

being myself.

Activity Time

- Is there anything in the list about feelings that someone does to me?
- How does that make me feel?
- Is it ok for an adult to do these things to me?

Tre always feels very uncomfortable visiting his dad's house because his step mum Talisha is so hard to live with. For some reason his dad thinks Talisha is super smart and funny, and never takes it seriously when Tre complains about her. Talisha has not got any kids of her own, and she wants Tre to do everything with her and Tre's dad "as a family." She really likes going on long hikes and even longer trips to craft markets and making Tre go with her.

He really dislikes hiking, and would rather use the weekend as a time to relax and play games. He hates the craft market trips even more, especially because it always involves long drives without his phone, because Talisha says it is family time.

Talisha often says things like "If you do not come along then your dad and I will be so upset. You are not respecting our feelings. You should be happy we care about you." Once Tre complained at the craft market that he was tired and hungry, and Talisha got upset and said "I try so hard to make you happy, but you always have to ruin everything! I love your dad so much but your behaviour makes me feel unwelcome. If we break up it is because of you!"

Activity Time

- Why are adult feelings the responsibility of adults?
- What can I tell myself when a Hard Adult tries to make me responsible for their feelings and behaviours?
- What could Talisha say instead to make Tre feel more welcome?
- Family time is important, but it can be organised in a caring way. If I was the parent how could I talk about it with a child so they feel comfortable?

Hard Adults can also use behaviours that are about controlling me in an unhealthy way. Some examples of these are:

- They might say they will hurt me or someone else, or say they will do something bad if I am not good enough.
- They may say I am lying when I am telling the truth.
- They may be very controlling of what I am allowed to do, and if I make mistakes they can get really upset.
- They can twist my words to mean something I did not

want.

- They could deliberately "forget" a birthday or other special event.
- They may use a special event to get attention and create issues with others around them.
- They tell me that something bad will happen to people I love if I do not listen to them.
- They do not say anything at all, using silence as a punishment.

Activity Time

- Is there anything in the list about controlling behaviour that someone does to me?
- How does that make me feel?
- Is it ok for an adult to do these things to me?

Carolina lives with her mum and grandma in a small town. Grandma is always worried about what other people think of them and say about them. She often threatens Carolina with things like "If you do not study hard enough I will be so embarrassed. Your mum had you young and is a failure, so you better do well or else!"

One day Carolina was not feeling well and wanted to stay home from school. Her mum was at work, and Grandma said she had to go to school because she had an important maths test. Carolina did her best at school that day even though she felt terrible, but unfortunately her test went badly. Grandma found out and she was furious. She said "Your bad behaviour is going to kill me! Forget about seeing your friends for the next month, you have to do extra studying to catch up. I do not care about your excuses."

Carolina thought it was super unfair and talked to her mum about it, who was annoyed about how strict Grandma was. When her mum talked with Grandma about it Grandma said "I did not say she cannot spend time with her friends. Carolina is sad about the test going badly, I am just supporting her with studying. Do not blame me for trying to help." Carolina thought maybe she remembered wrong and Grandma was right, but she felt like Grandma was sneaky with her words, twisting things to make herself look better.

Activity Time

- Why is it bad for people to use threats to get other people to do what they want?
- What can I do if a Hard Adult twists their words to try to get what they want?
- How can I explain the word twisting to a Safe Adult?

There might be someone in my life who asks me to do activities that I should not do. There might be things that I think are normal to do, but other kids don't. There could be some things that I am made to do that make me uncomfortable. Here are a few examples of what Hard Adults might ask kids to do:

- They expect me to support **them** instead of them supporting **me**.
- They ask me to keep bad secrets.
- They ask me to stay by myself for a long time, or to look after my siblings while they leave the house for a long time.
- They ask me to do things that should be the job of adults.
- They want me to feed myself because they do not feel like preparing food. I may not have anything to eat at all.
- They make me spend time with people I feel very uncomfortable with.
- They do not take me to the doctor or give me medicine when I am sick.
- They sometimes do not take me to school, sports practice, or other events that I usually do.

Activity Time

- Is there anything in the list of activities that someone does to me?
- How does that make me feel?
- Is it ok for an adult to do these things to me?
- Do I have a Hard Adult in my life?

Example

Pria always felt very alone, even when she was surrounded by others. She was the eldest of four children and they lived with just their dad who worked long days at a company. Because Pria was the oldest she often got stuck doing jobs that she should not have to do. If one of her siblings got sick then Pria had to skip school to look after them because her dad was at work.

Pria was also left to do most of the cooking and cleaning in the house, and she felt like she had to be an adult when really she just wanted to have fun like all the other children.

One day she was really tired and complained to her dad about how much work she has to do. He said "Can you not see how hard I am working? You should appreciate me more. Do not tell your siblings, but the company is not doing well, and I am afraid I will lose my job if I do not work extra hours."

Activity Time

- Children have the right to an education. Why is this important?
- Should Pria's dad have told her about the problems at the company? Why, why not?
- Why is it so important for adults to look after children properly?

One of the very serious things that a Hard Adult may ask is to do with my body. It is important to know that my body is mine, and people should not touch me unless I am comfortable. For example, I do not have to hug someone if I do not want to. Safe Adults will always keep healthy boundaries with my body, and that is one of the big reasons I feel safe with them.

Hard Adults might pay a lot of attention to my body, make uncomfortable comments about it, or try to touch me in ways I do not like. They might try sweet talking me into letting them do it, or make me feel guilty so they get what they want. They might start out with something that does not feel bad, but ask me to do worse and worse things as time goes on. They might not even touch me, just talk about what they want to do to me. It might not even be me who they are doing this to, but someone else in my family, and I know about it.

Hard Adults know that their behaviour is very bad, so they will not want other adults find out about it. Because they are afraid and ashamed of others finding out, they will come up with powerful threats to keep me quiet. For example, they could say "If you tell anyone, then you will not get to see your mum anymore." Or they could say "If you tell, then everyone will think it is your fault and nobody will love you anymore."

The truth is, I am not the one doing the wrong thing- they are! In fact, there are strong laws made by world governments that say that this sort of behaviour is illegal. By telling Safe Adults about this I am **not** doing anything wrong, and there are lots of adults out there who want to help me. I am not the one who should be afraid and ashamed, only the Hard Adult. It is **always** ok to talk about this with someone I trust.

Practice Saying

- The threats and untruths of Hard Adults are not healthy, and I am allowed to talk about them with Safe Adults.
- My body is my own. I respect myself.
- I have the right to feel safe

At this stage in the book I already have a really good understanding about who Safe Adults and Hard Adults are, what sort of things they do, how they make me feel, and what sort of things they ask me to do. The rest of this book looks at some useful information about my relationships with Safe and Hard Adults.

First, I am going to learn about something called trauma, which is all about how my body responds to difficult situations. Then I am going to learn more about love and what it really is. There is also a chapter about some of the more complicated Hard Adult behaviours and how to recognise them. And finally, there is going to be a whole chapter about how I can help myself and how to ask for help from others.

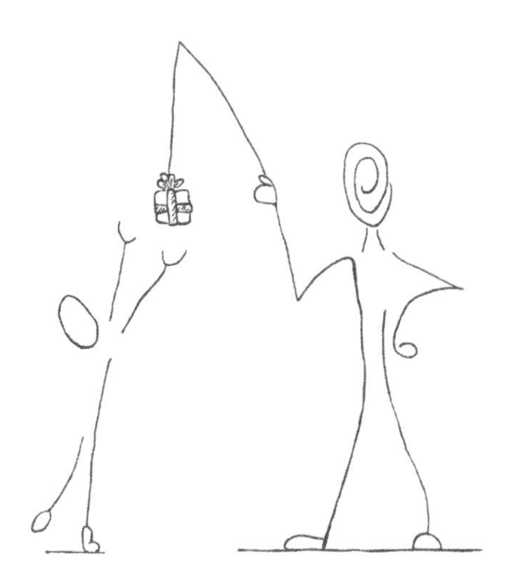

Chapter 4

How My Body Behaves

There are four ways that a person's body can react when something really bad happens to them. They are called fight, flight, freeze and fawn. Sometimes I might do one and other days another, and it is ok to do these things, because it is the natural way my body behaves when I am scared. Everybody does these things, even the bravest adults.

Fight makes me feel like fighting back against someone who has hurt me or someone else. It makes me feel like punching or shouting and using my body a lot. My fingers might shake, and I feel full of energy. I can feel my heart beating fast as I look for a way to physically protect myself (or others).

Flight makes me feel like running away somewhere safe. I do not want to be near the scary stuff at all. My legs may feel like jelly, my heart can beat really fast, and I will think about how I can escape. I may be full of fear and think about all the ways I can get out of there.

Freeze makes me wish I could be invisible. It becomes hard to move my body, talk, and to think about what I should do. I feel like when the bad thing happens I have no control at all. My heart may be beating fast, and I may feel frozen or stuck.

Fawning makes me feel like I have to be extra good so the Hard Adult will be nice to me. I do what they ask even if I am just pretending to be ok. On the outside I am really good, but on the inside I am scared. I feel like I have to be perfect so they will love me and not punish me or ignore me.

Activity Time

- Think about a time that I was really scared- how did I behave? What did my body feel like?
- When I am around a Hard Adult does my body react in any of these ways? Which ones?
- Sometimes I may react in these ways even if nothing bad has happened right then. It can be caused by a memory, stress, sudden noise, and other things. Has that happened to me? What caused it to happen?

When something terrible happens to me and I feel the effects of it for a long time afterwards it could be something called trauma. Trauma happens inside everyone, even the strongest and bravest people. It is ok to have trauma, and I can talk about it with my Safe Adults. But what does trauma look like? It is a bit different for everyone, but here are a few things that can happen:

My body can feel very tight, it can be hard to breathe, my heart can beat too fast, or I can have too much energy and feel out of control. I could also have a sore tummy, heaviness or pain in my heart, or dizziness in my head. I could have trouble sleeping and have nightmares. My feelings can get confused as well. I might worry a lot, have sad thoughts, and struggle with making decisions.

It is possible to get fearful and panic about things that would usually not affect me, have sudden bad memories or dreams, become forgetful, and even feel like the world is unreal.

It can make it hard for me to control my emotions and have healthy relationships. It can also lead to eating disorders, self-harm, and addictions to things like food, alcohol, and drugs. Trauma can take over my life and make me feel worthless and helpless. If I have any of these thoughts or feelings I can talk about it with a Safe Adult. I can use this book to help explain what is going on with me. I am **not** alone, I **deserve** to feel better, and there **is** help available.

Feelings are my reaction to the world around me. For example, if I look at a cute video about animals it can bring me joy. If someone screams horrible things at me it can cause me to feel sad and angry. I am not naturally angry and unhappy, it is just the feelings visiting me in a difficult moment. Unfortunately, those bad feelings can end up sticking around when I do not want them to.

Traumas are bad feelings and memories that have stuck with me, and it can sometimes feel like they are going to stay forever. Being able to recognise and let go of bad feelings and memories is part of the process of healing. I do not want trauma to control my life. Luckily I am not alone with this, and now I have a better understanding of how Hard Adults behave and how trauma works. I can make a plan with my Safe Adults about how I can heal.

Sometimes having a positive relationship with a Hard Adult becomes impossible. They cannot hold a safe and loving relationship, and the result is that we cannot be together. I deserve to have healthy relationships with the people around me, and I deserve to be safe.

There can be a feeling of loss and grief about missing out on a positive relationship with the Hard Adult, even if that positive connection is long gone or was never there. It is normal to feel grief about a lost relationship, and it can take a while to heal.

Activity Time

- Think about times I have been really scared or stressed-what sort of reaction did I have?
- How do I sleep after a bad day?
- How does my body feel after a fight?

- How clear are my thoughts afterwards, and what are am I focused on?
- What sort of hard feelings have I had recently? What was happening when I felt those feelings?
- What feelings of loss or grief have I felt about a Hard Adult?
- What activities bring me positive feelings?

Practice Saying

- The bad things I feel do not make me a bad person.
- Feelings are not a part of me, and I can choose to accept them or let them go.
- It is normal to have trauma and I can heal from it.
- It is ok to talk about trauma and it is ok to ask for help.

One of the most important things along my journey to healing from trauma is good relationships. This can be with family, friends, carers, teachers, mentors; whoever is part of my support system. Having healthy relationships with people who care about me can give me positive experiences and more joyful meaning to life. Healthy relationships help me feel loved, accepted, and understood.

Reading this book together with a Safe Adult is already helping me, but there are lots of other things I can do for myself as well, even when a Safe Adult may not be there. Moving my body makes my brain happy, so going for a walk, playing sport, or even doing star jumps or yoga in my room will help me feel better.

I need to be honest with myself about how I am feeling, and if the answer is that I do not feel good, then adding in exercise (even just 10 minutes in the morning) can give me a big boost.

If I am feeling anxious and having trouble breathing I can splash cold water on my face. This helps reset my brain to be more calm. Another way to feel better about myself is through helping others. I can see if I can help out with something positive in my family or with a community or school event. By helping others I can help myself.

I can also explore some hobbies that can bring me joy, for example singing, gardening, photography, drawing, writing, dancing- there are a lot to choose from.

Activity Time

- Who can I talk with to help me feel loved, accepted, and understood?
- What physical exercise do I enjoy doing?
- What other activities help me feel calm, happy, and safe?
- What family and community events are happening around me?

At this stage in the book I already have a really good understanding about who Safe Adults and Hard Adults are, and I can use the things I have learned about here to understand how my body responds to the trauma that I have gone through. It is important to remember that I am not responsible for the trauma that I have gone through, but I am responsible for myself, and how I can heal and grow after it has happened.

I can choose each day to make little positive changes that will turn into big positive outcomes over time. I have control over my own body and mind, and I can ask for help from a Safe Adult if it feels too big or too overwhelming for me.

Chapter 5

The Thing Called Love

People say "I love you!" all the time- in movies, in books, and in real life. But what does it really mean? There are some things that are included in love, and some things that are not.

I **can** feel love, but love is not **just** a feeling. When I really love someone (and when someone really loves me) it is actually all about how we behave with each other. Someone cannot just say they love me and then do things that hurt me or make me feel unsafe, because that means their words and actions do not match. Someone might buy me gifts because they think buying me stuff will make me like them more, but love cannot be bought. Real love is shown through reliable actions over time.

Sometimes love is messy. It includes having hard conversations (like in this book) with the people I care about and being honest about how I feel. The people who love me will keep loving me through the messy times, and the hard things I am going through do not make them love me less. Sometimes Safe Adults have to deal with problems, but I can see in the way they behave that it is more important for them to show love than it is to win an argument. They care less about winning than about caring for me and themselves.

Hard Adults are a bit trickier. Everyone is born with a heart that can love, but some people's hearts have a love-shaped-hole in them. This hole usually happens when they are kids or teenagers. That means that the Hard Adult in my life got the hole in their heart **before** I was even born. It is not my fault that they have that hole.

It may not be their fault either. They probably had a Hard Adult in their life, or some other terrible thing happened to make the hole grow. That does not mean that the hard way they behave is ever ok, but this helps it make sense. Most Hard Adults do not even know that the hole is there! I am not responsible for telling a Hard Adult about the love-shaped-hole, fixing the hole, or trying to fill it up. **That is an adult responsibility**.

Hard Adults can find it hard to love others and deep down they do not really love themselves either (although their selfish behaviour may make it look like they love themselves a lot). I want them to love me, but they do not work like that. This is probably the hardest part of Hard Adults- I want their love and kindness but they are unable to give it to me, and that is very sad. It is ok to be sad about it and have other big feelings, too.

The good news is that I do not **need** their love. That may be surprising, but it is true. Not everyone who is around me loves me, and I cannot make anyone love me. Nobody can!

There is a big question though- if Hard Adults got a hole in their hearts because they were hurt by other Hard Adults, then will I become a Hard Adult because they are hurting me? Well, the good news is that I have the secret weapon to stop that from happening. It might sound a bit cheesy, but the secret weapon against getting the hole is love. I can love myself even though I may not be perfect. I can love and accept others with their imperfections. I can accept that the only person I can change is myself.

My job is to make me the best version of myself, growing things like patience, kindness, and self-control. I can focus on how I see myself instead of worrying about how others see me. A wise man called Mr. Rogers once said that "knowing that we can be loved exactly as we are gives us all the best opportunity for growing into the healthiest of people." I can choose to focus on the loving relationships in my life, and to love myself as well. **No matter what, I deserve love**.

Another wise man called Dr. Martin Luther King once said that "darkness cannot drive out darkness; only light can do that. Hate cannot drive out hate; only love can do that." What he meant was using anger to get back at someone, or using anger and bitterness to protect myself will not end up well. I have to learn to let go of the anger and focus on showing myself and those close to me as much love as possible.

Love is what builds strong friendships and relationships, and that is what will bring me the most joy. It can be really hard to let go of anger (for Safe Adults as well), but it is something we can work on together.

Activity Time

- Think about someone important in my life who loves me. What do they do to show their love?
- When I feel sad about a Hard Adult not giving me the love I need what is a healthy thing I can do to feel better?
- What are my favourite actions to show someone I love them?

One of the most famous things ever written about love comes from the book called the Bible, in a part called 1 Corinthians, verses 4-8:

> Love is patient and kind, and never jealous, proud, or rude. Love is not selfish or quick to anger. It does not focus on the wrong things that other people do. Love finds joy in the truth, but not in bad things. Love is always supportive, loyal, hopeful, and trusting. Love never fails!

Activity Time

- How is this similar to what I have learned about Safe Adults and Hard Adults?
- What loving things do I do well with others?
- How could I show more love towards myself?

Practice saying

- I deserve love from the adults in my life.
- I love myself, and I accept myself as I am.
- Real love shows in actions over time.
- No matter how messy my life is, I deserve love.

Love is a really important part of life, and now I know that love is a mix of lots of actions that people do. Safe Adults usually try their best to show love through their actions, but Hard Adults aren't always able to do a good job of showing love because of the love shaped hole in their heart.

I do not need love from everyone to be worthy of love, and I can choose to focus on the love I get from Safe Adults, friends, and others who really care for me. No matter what, I deserve love.

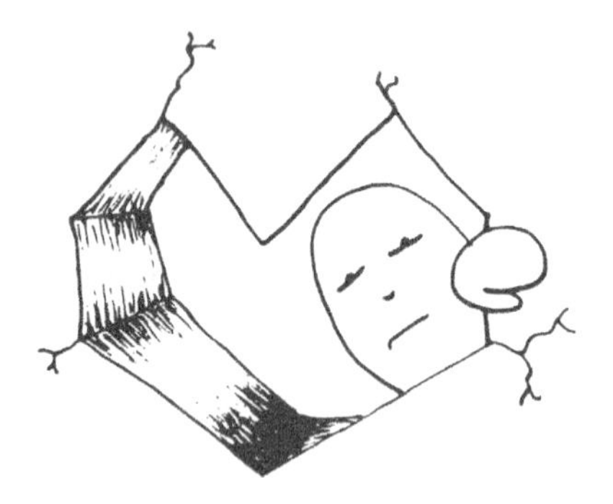

Chapter 6

Going Forward

I have now learned a lot about my relationships with Safe Adults and Hard Adults and it is time to use that knowledge to make my life better. Here are two really important lists. The first is about things I can remember in life that can help me think in a healthy way about myself and about my relationships. The second is about things that I can do to stay safe, get help, and feel better in myself.

REMEMBER

- I am loved, I deserve love.
- My voice is important, and it is ok to tell Safe Adults the truth.
- The difficult things a Hard Adult does are not my fault.
- I can love a Hard Adult and still dislike their bad behaviour.
- Safe Adults are doing everything they can to keep me safe.

- It is ok to say 'NO' and 'STOP' to things about my body.
- It is always ok to ask for help.
- It is always ok to cry.
- It is not my job to fix a Hard Adult.
- It is not my job to make a Hard Adult happy.
- It is ok to be myself. I do not have to change to make others happy.
- It is ok to make mistakes.
- I do not have to be perfect to be a good person who deserves love.
- Adults should treat me, others, and themselves with respect.
- An adult's words and behaviours should match up.

DO

- I can talk to Safe Adults about any problems with a Hard Adult.
- I can draw or write down things a Hard Adult does so I can remember it and tell a Safe Adult.
- I can be open and honest with Safe Adults, not keeping any bad secrets or worries.
- I can tell people I trust who the Hard Adult in my life is. I can use this book to help explain what the Hard Adult does to me, how they make me feel, and what they make me do.
- I can make a list of activities with a Safe Adult that help me relax and feel safe and happy. Singing, dancing to music, playing sport, deep breathing, going for a walk, talking to a friend, volunteering- there are lots of things I can try.
- Ask a Safe Adult to help me practice some activities that help me relax and feel better.
- If I am really stressed and cannot breathe well I can splash my face with cold water to help me calm down.
- When I am panicking, I can remember to take 5 deep breaths and think of 4 things I can see, 3 things I can touch, 2 things I can hear, and 1 thing I can smell.

- I can choose to refuse to get involved with situations that make me uncomfortable.

Something that everyone wants in their life is control. It feels good when people do what I want them to do, and it also feels good to be able to do whatever I want to do. But the truth about control is that some things are things I **can** control, and some things which are **out** of my control. Here is a picture showing the two:

I *can* control

My boundaries

My thoughts and actions

My goals

How I speak to myself

What I choose to think about

I *cannot* control

The past

The future

How others behave

What other people think

What other people think of me

What happens around me

The things I can't control are the same for adults, too. Safe Adults usually understand the things they cannot control (but they may not like it very much), but Hard Adults do not want to accept that they are not in control of everything. **When they feel out of control is when they behave the worst.** I do not want to be like that, so I am going to concentrate on the things that I can control.

What goes on in my own mind and heart are in my control, and I can look after them like a garden. If I plant negative thoughts and feelings about myself, my future, and my relationships then that is what will grow and grow. If I choose to have positive goals, and kind thoughts and actions towards others and myself, then I can grow a loving heart.

Activity Time

- What positive thoughts and actions can I concentrate on today?
- What positive goals can I have for myself?
- What sorts of things can I say to myself when I am feeling down?
- When I am dealing with a lot of difficult things what helps me cheer up? What can I focus on to get me through the tough moments?

For now, I may not have a choice about being near a Hard Adult. The good news is that the older I get the more choices I will have about who I spend time with. I might decide that even though a Hard Adult in my life is difficult to be around I still want to spend time with them, and that is ok. It is also ok to say that I do not want to see them regularly, or at all.

I do not have to give them a reason for not wanting to spend time together- that is my personal choice, but if there are court orders or something similar in place then I need to be able to speak up about my opinion to people like lawyers, police officers, and a judge. It is useful to think about what I want to say to them so they can have a clear idea about how I feel and what I have experienced. I can use this book to get my thoughts together.

Asking for help can feel difficult because of being scared about what will happen next. I may be worried about what people will think or say, and that is ok. I can ask for help from a Safe Adult, police, social workers, doctors, teachers at school, and other safe adults. It is their job to find me the best help I can get. I can use this book to help explain what is happening to me.

There are also special adults who can help me with trauma and they are called counsellors, therapists, psychologists, and psychiatrists. These are fancy names that all mean one important thing: they know how feelings work and their job is to help me feel better, and keep me safe. Sometimes my Safe Adult will take me to see someone who can help me with my difficult feelings and worries, and I can use what I learned in this book to explain to them what is going on.

There may be times when I have to talk to adults I do not know about the Hard Adult. For example, a police officer or a social worker could have some questions for me. They may ask about a specific thing, or just ask me to say what I want. I can do my best to tell them:

- Who was there when it happened
- What happened
- When it happened
- Where it happened
- How it made me feel

Activity Time

- List at least three Safe Adults- one at home, one at school, and one somewhere else, in a table with their contact details.
- What is the number for police? Write down a sentence I can use when I call them. Hi my name is ... My address is ... My emergency is ...
- What is a number for a children's support line in my area?

- Pretend I am asking for their help on the phone now. What do I say?

- What are the things on the "Do" list that give me confidence?

- What are the things on the "Remember" list that are most important to me?

I can remember that Hard Adults are often hard with other people too, and not just me. Sometimes Safe Adults also have problems with Hard Adults, so they understand what I am going through. Safe Adults will do what they can to protect me from Hard Adults. This may mean that they need to listen to police, social workers, and court orders even if they do not agree with the decisions.

Sometimes the decisions made in court or by other adults feel really unfair. It is ok to be sad and angry about it, and Safe Adults may feel really upset too, but they have to follow whatever rules have been made.

Choices made by the court (usually by a judge) are very powerful and hard to change, but the older I get the stronger my voice will be and the more choices I will have. There are probably more difficulties going on for the Safe Adult, but they choose not to share that information with me because they understand that it is an adult problem, and they know that I have enough hard stuff to deal with without having to worry about those as well.

One of the more practical things that I can do directly with Hard Adults is to create boundaries with them. Will they like it when I do this? No, probably not, so first I have to know that I will be physically safe. If I feel safe enough to do so, I can start with a simple boundary about myself. For example, "I am feeling tired. I would like to rest on my own for a bit." I am not asking the Hard Adult to do anything for me or with me, they do not have to do anything to make this boundary happen.

I can also try to make boundaries about my body. For example "I do not feel like giving kisses and hugs when we meet. Can we please do a fist pump instead?" I am saying clearly what I do not like, and I offer something else instead, but the Hard Adult might not like it because it is not what they wanted to do.

If it is safe to do so, I can say this every time we meet and hopefully they will learn to accept how important it is for me. The most difficult boundaries for Hard Adults to accept are those that make them feel hurt.

For example, "I do not like the way you yell at me and throw my stuff around, please stop doing that." It is a very good boundary, and it is ok to ask for it, but a Hard Adult might think to themselves "This kid is trying to boss me around. I'll show them who is boss!" and they may react badly. Hard Adults can take boundaries very personally, so learning to have boundaries with them will always be hard work.

Activity Time

- How have I tried to make boundaries with a Hard Adult in the past?
- Brainstorm some boundaries I would like to have in the future.
- Practice saying boundaries in a polite but firm way.
- Think about how I can stay positive and safe if a Hard Adult refuses to accept a boundary.

A very important thing I can do to make life better for myself is something called self-care. Doing little things like having a regular shower, brushing my teeth, and keeping my room tidy can help me feel better. Getting enough sleep, eating healthy, and exercise also really help. Spending many hours a day on devices does not help, and can actually make me more sad and moody.

Listening to music, singing, playing sport, enjoying nature, and hanging out with friends and family or other Safe Adults can all really help me be more positive. I can make a plan with a Safe Adult about how to fit self-care into my life so that I can feel better tomorrow than I do today. Hard Adults can put a shadow over my life with their behaviour, but using my self-care strategies and the support from Safe Adults can help the shadow get smaller.

Activity Time

- What can I do to get enough sleep?
- What sort of sports can I do?
- How can I remind myself every day about keeping myself and my area clean?
- What activities make me happy, and how can I fit them into my life?
- Who can I do these activities with?
- Why is self-care important to me?
- What sort of self-care activity can I do together with others?

Now I understand much more about the difference between Safe Adults and Hard Adults. I know that trauma can make big feelings happen, and that it is ok to have those feelings. I have a list of activities I can do to help me feel better when I am upset. I have my list of things to **remember** and **do** to help me when things are hard.

I know who I can talk to if something bad happens or if there is an emergency. Most importantly, I know that my Safe Adults love me, and I am not alone in finding a good way forward in my life together with people who care about me.

Chapter 7
Conclusion

I have reached the last chapter of the book! I have done so well to read it, learn about serious topics, and learn how to talk about them with others. This is a tough book to read and understand, and I should be very proud of myself for getting through it. In this chapter I can read through the main ideas that I learned about in the other chapters so that I can remember them and talk about them comfortably.

In chapter one I learned about how Safe Adults and Hard Adults behave. There are some big differences! Can I remember 3 things Safe Adults do? Can I remember 3 things Hard Adults do? People's actions tell me a lot about how they think and feel. Safe Adult's words and actions will usually make sense, and I feel safe around them.

Hard Adult's behaviours often do not respect my feelings, my body, and my stuff and other people's bodies, feelings, and stuff. Safe Adults usually take responsibility for their words and actions, while Hard Adults do not.

In chapter two I learned how to look at my own feelings to figure out who are Safe Adults and who are Hard Adults. Can I remember 3 way that Safe Adults make me feel? Can I remember 3 ways that Hard Adults might make me feel? Learning about my own feelings has helped me to trust my instincts, and decide who is a Safe Adult and who is not.

I also learned that my feelings are not part of who I am, and that I am in control of my own feelings (but nobody else's).

Chapter three was all about what adults ask me to do. Can I remember 3 things that Safe Adults could ask me? Can I remember 3 things that Hard Adults may ask me to do? I learned that adult feelings and responsibilities were not mine to solve, and that using bad feelings to make me do things is not ok.

Hard Adults can be controlling with words and actions, and they can have strong emotional reactions when things do not go their way. I also learned that my body is my own, it is special, and deserves respect.

In chapter four the main topic was trauma. I learned about how my body behaves when trauma happens (fight, flight, freeze, and fawn), and about the sorts of feelings I can have in my body because of trauma. I know that these problems can become quite serious, and they do not just disappear if I ignore them.

This is something I will need to work on, but thankfully I am not alone in doing that. Having trauma is **never** my fault, and I am the one in control of healing myself, together with those who care about me.

Love was the topic in chapter five. The major point is that love is about actions and not just words and promises. Love is the hard work that people put in no matter their difficulties in life because that is how much they care about me. Sometimes love includes having difficult conversations, and helping each other through the hard times.

One of the saddest parts about Hard Adults is that they find it hard to give and accept love. The good news is that I can focus on loving myself, and loving the people around me who care about me. I am only responsible for the things in my control, and that is my own heart, mind, and actions.

Chapter six is about putting all things I have learned in this book into action. Can I recall 3 things on the "Remember" list? Can I recall 3 things on the "Do" list? I also learned that some things are in my control, and some things are not. Can I think of 3 things that I am in control of today? I have a good plan for emergencies, I know who the Safe Adults in my life are and that I am not alone with my thoughts and feelings.

Life with a Hard Adult around can make things more complicated, but now I have a better understanding about the difference between Safe Adults and Hard Adults, and I am able to talk about my problems a lot clearer. This is just the start- I can continue learning about myself and others, seeking healing and having a voice.

Chapter 8
Extra Materials

There are some habits that Hard Adults have that I might see happening. They may involve me, or it may be other family members, partners, friends, or other people. It is useful for me to know about these, so I can make sense of the behaviour of the Hard Adult and to also understand the reactions of others around them. I understand that Hard Adults choose to behave like this, and no matter what, these sort of behaviours are **never** my fault. To make things easier, here are some terms that adults use, and the meaning behind them.

The Cycle of Abuse

Often Hard Adults will behave in a certain pattern that has four steps to it. The first step is where they behave in a very loving and caring way, giving gifts and compliments. When this happens I start to see the Hard Adult as kind and trustworthy. In the second stage, I already expect them to be kind, and their opinion matters to me.

They start to change their behaviour, stopping kind actions, and becoming more controlling.

The third stage is the hardest, where all the Hard Adult behaviours that I have learned about can really show up. When this happens it is normal for me to start to distrust them, and go through the trauma responses that I learned about (fight, flight, freeze, and fawn). The Hard Adult will notice my behaviour changing, but they do not want to lose their control, so they will go into phase four, which is trying to get me to trust them again.

This often involves them apologising (but only to get me back, not for real), acting kind again, and they make promises about how good the future will be. Often they will also say how the bad things that happened were my fault, and that they are the one that has been hurt and not me. This cycle is something that they will do with Safe Adults as well.

Activity Time

- Think about my relationship with the Hard Adult. Have I been through the cycle before? Have any of my Safe Adults been through this?
- Brainstorm ideas with a Safe Adult about how to help me deal with all four parts of the cycle.

The Golden Child and Scapegoat

When there is a home with more than one child, the Hard Adult may have a favourite child (or children). Usually it is a kid who does what the Hard Adult wants. That kid did not choose to be the favourite, and the way the Hard Adult treats them as special is not their fault. Often these kids are stuck in the trauma response of fawning, as a way to protect themselves.

That means they behave in the way they think the Hard Adult will like, even if that is not really how they want to behave. They are scared of the Hard Adult, and they do whatever they need to do to be as safe as possible. They are behaving in a way that protects them, fitting in with what the Hard Adult wants.

On the other hand, there may be a child (or children) in the family who is mistreated by the Hard Adult. This can include a few things:

- They are completely ignored.
- The Hard Adult does not consider their basic needs (like food, clothing, safety, and love).
- The Hard Adult blames that child for things they did not do.
- The Hard Adult bullies that child.
- They blame them for the bad things that **they** do.

It is never my fault if a Hard Adult treats me like this. Everyone is responsible for their own behaviour. It is not my fault if I do not fawn and act like they want me to. I am allowed to have healthy boundaries and stick to them, and the Safe Adults in my life are also allowed to stick to their healthy boundaries.

Activity Time

- How am I treated by the Hard Adult in my life?
- Do I fawn around a Hard Adult? What about my siblings?
- How might others feel who are treated differently from me?
- How can I show kindness to others in this situation?

No matter how the Hard Adult treats me, it is important to remember that my value as a person is not something they can change. **I know how valuable I am.**

Smear Campaign

Sometimes Hard Adults will be so full of hard feelings that they tell lies to make themselves feel better and stronger. This can include things like telling untruths about me and other family members. In some cases, Hard Adults will tell untruths about me to someone else to get a Safe Adult in trouble or to control a situation. This is not ok, and it is ok to find another adult I trust to talk about this.

This sort of situation is never my fault, and it is always ok to talk, especially if a Hard Adult says to keep it a secret.

Secrets that are made to hurt other people are not secrets that I need to keep. It can become really hard to know the difference between truths and lies, especially when I love the people involved in the situation. At these times it is good to go back to chapter 5 and remind myself that love is about long-term actions, and not words or tricks to get me to do something.

I can pay careful attention to see how the adults around me behave, and use that to make decisions. It is also a good time to find an adult to help me who is not involved in the situation.

Activity Time

- Has anyone around me used lies to get what they want? Talk about how it happened and what made me realise it was wrong.
- What is a healthier way to ask for help?
- What can I do to help myself feel better when I am upset?

Grey Rock Technique

Hard Adults are hard for other adults to deal with and not just me. Sometimes Hard Adults can be so difficult to be around that other adults prefer not to talk to them much, or at all. And that is ok. Sometimes it is better to let relationships rest instead of continuing arguments and creating more pain. Safe Adults sometimes need to put barriers in place so the Hard Adult cannot keep hurting them.

Not talking to someone sounds easy, but it also means that if a Hard Adult is yelling, bullying, and being a maximum powered Hard Adult, the Safe Adult will still say nothing. It can take a lot of strength to remain calm and not argue back. They choose not to reply to the nasty behaviour, and they will leave when they can.

It can be a lot more tricky when they are thinking about the safety of children as well, and it may mean they need to talk to the Hard Adult more often than is comfortable, but that is the sort of responsibility Safe Adults take on to keep me safe.

I can also choose to stay quiet when a Hard Adult is bullying me. If I show no interest in them, they will hopefully leave me alone. However, I should always speak up to Safe Adults about what is going on so they can continue helping me.

Activity Time

- Talk with a Safe Adult about how they protect themselves from the behaviour of a Hard Adult
- In what sort of situation is it better to stay quiet with a Hard Adult?
- When is it really important to speak up?

Understanding different types of behaviour is useful for me so that I can avoid getting mixed up in it. Behaviours have patterns, and I now understand them better.

Key Questions from the Book:

Questions from Chapter 1 "Things They Do"

- Who helps me with my feelings and worries?
- Who helps me be seen, heard, and understood?
- How do they show me they love me?
- How do I know I can trust them?
- How do they behave when I tell them about my worries?
- How do they behave when I do something wrong?
- Is there anyone in my life who behaves in a Hard way?
- How do they behave when I tell them about my worries?
- How do they behave when I do something wrong?
- How does their behaviour make me feel?

Questions from Chapter 2 "How They Make Me Feel"

- What do my Safe Adults do to make me feel safe?
- What do my Safe Adults do to make me feel happy?
- What do my Safe Adults do to make me feel loved?
- What has happened to make me feel confused, scared or angry?
- What has happened to make me feel shame or guilt?
- What do I usually do when I am feeling these bad feelings?
- What do I do to avoid problems with the Hard Adult?
- What is stopping me from talking about all these feelings with a Safe Adult?

Questions from Chapter 3 "What They Ask Me to Do"

- Who are the Safe Adults in my life?
- What do they do that helps me know they are really safe for me?
- How do Safe Adults respond when I do not do as they ask?
- Why shouldn't people use threats to get other people to do what they want?
- What can I do if a Hard Adult twists their words to get what they want?
- What do Hard Adults ask me to do that I do not feel good about?

Questions from Chapter 4 "How My Body Behaves"

- Think about a time that I was really scared- how did I behave?
- When I am around a Hard Adult does my body react in any of these ways? Which ones?
- Sometimes I may do these even if nothing has happened, I could just think there is danger. Has that happened to me? When did it happen?
- Think about times I have been really scared or stressed- what sort of reaction did I have?
- How do I sleep after a bad day?
- How does my body feel after a fight?
- How clear are my thoughts afterwards, and what are am I focused on?
- Who can I talk with to help me feel loved, accepted, and understood?
- What physical exercise do I enjoy doing?
- What other activities help me feel calm, happy, and safe?
- What family and community events are happening around

me?

Australian Contact Numbers

Police emergency 000

Police non-emergency 131-444

1800RESPECT 1800-737-732 Domestic Violence support

Kids Helpline 1800-551-800 Mental health support

Beyond Blue 1300-224 636 Mental health support

Lifeline 13-11-14

Aboriginal & Torres Strait Islander crisis support line 13YARN13-92-76

Suicide Call Back Service 1300-659-467

Canadian Contact Numbers

Police emergency 911

Police non-emergency 311

Kids' Help Phone: 1-800-668-6868 or text CONNECT to 686868

Youth Mental Health Canada https://ymhc.ngo/

Talk Suicide Canada at 1-833-456-4566

Wellness Together Canada 1-888-668-6810 or text WELLNESS to 686868

For First Nations, Inuit, and Métis Peoples, Hope for Wellness Help Line 1-855-242-3310

New Zealand Contact Numbers

Police emergency 111

Police non-emergency 105

Youthline 0800 37 66 33 or text 234

The Low Down 0800-111-757 or text 5626.

Whatsup? 0800-942-8787. Talkline

1737 is a free national counselling service

The Suicide Crisis Line 0508 TAUTOKO 0508-828-865

United Kingdom Contact Numbers

Police emergency 999 and 112

Police non-emergency 101

Samaritans 116-123 Talkline for everyone

Samaritans Welsh Language Line 0808-164-0123

National Domestic Abuse Helpine, England 0808-2000-247

Domestic and Sexual Abuse Helpline, Northern Ireland 0808-802-1414

Domestic Abuse and Forced Marriage Helpline, Scotland 0800-027-1234

Live Fear Free, Wales 0808-80-10-800

HOPELINEUK on 0800-068-4141. Talking for kids and teens.

The Mix 0808-808-4994. Talkline for young people

National Suicide Prevention Helpline UK on 0800-689-5652

kidscape.org.ukfor bullying and abuse

United States of America Contact Numbers

Police emergency 911

Police non-emergency 311

National Domestic Violence Hotline 1 (800) 799 – 7233

Love Is Respect- National Teen Dating Abuse Hotline Hotline: 1 (866) 331 – 9474, Text: 22522

Strong Hearts Native Helpline 1 (844) 762 – 8483

Child Help National Child Abuse Hotline 1 (800) 422 – 4453

National Suicide Prevention Lifeline 1-800-273-8255

National Suicide Prevention Spanish Speaking 1-888-628-9454

Acknowledgements

Friends are blessings, and I am privileged to have some truly amazing souls in my life.

Thank you to Kaitlyn Rasmussen for your design work, editing, and emotional support. You beautifully reinterpreted my crayon chicken scribble idea for the cover, and you patiently edited the first draft. You have been my artistic sounding board as I have slowly figured out the details of self-publishing. I am eternally grateful.

Many thanks to Lynlee Brytan for your meticulous feedback from a social worker's perspective. You read my very first dot points several years ago and helped me believe that it can become something greater. Your patience and pragmatic wisdom have been invaluable.

A big thank you to Caitlin Tyler and Amy Shipway for the eleventh hour proof reading.

I would also like to acknowledge the work of all the wonderful psychologists and therapists who have influenced my understanding on the topics covered in this book. I humbly stand on the shoulders of giants with brilliant hearts and minds.

Bessel Van Der Kolk, author of "The Body Keeps The Score"

Brook Olsen, on "The High Conflict Co-Parenting Podcast"

Dr Les Carter, on the "Surviving Narcissism" YouTube channel

Dr Nicole LePera, aka "The Holistic Psychologist" on Facebook and Instagram

Dr Ramani Durvasula, on the DoctorRamani YouTube channel

Fjelstad and McBride, authors of "Raising Resilient Children with a Borderline or Narcissistic Parent"

Lisa A Romano, on the "Breakdown to Breakthrough" podcast

Lundy Bancroft, author of "Why Does He Do That?"

Thank you also to my beautiful family, both biological and spiritual. The last few years have been incredibly testing, and I could not be where I am today without the emotional support and day-to-day assistance from you all.

Finally, thanks to all the wonderful souls I have had the privilige of talking with -both on social media and in person- whose stories have motivated me to keep writing. Working on a book like this can be really emotionally draining, but you have kept inspiring me again and again to keep going. It is finished because of you, and for you. Thank you.

Made in the USA
Middletown, DE
13 February 2024